Better Than It Sounds

The music teacher came twice each week to bridge
the awful gap between Dorothy and Chopin.
— **George Ade**

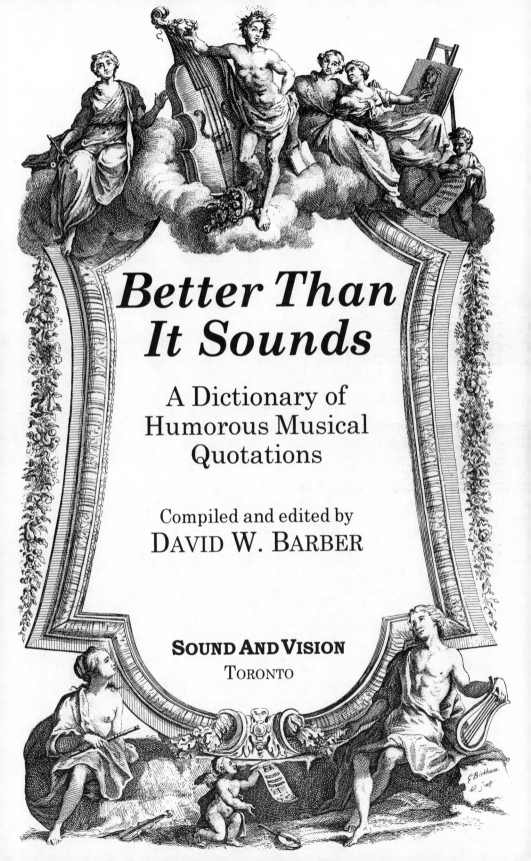

Better Than It Sounds

A Dictionary of Humorous Musical Quotations

Compiled and edited by
DAVID W. BARBER

SOUND AND VISION

TORONTO

Editor's Note

Having spent a good deal of my time trying to come up with funny things to say about music, I decided it was time to take a little break (some break!) and let others say the funny stuff.

There are hundreds of quotes here by, for and about musicians. In some cases I've stretched that definition a bit, I'll admit. (Frost's remark that "Hell is a half-filled auditorium" isn't specifically about music, but musicians will certainly be able to relate. Likewise for several of the remarks about critics.)

Wherever possible, I've tried to give proper attribution to and information about the authors of these remarks, but that hasn't always been easy, since many other lexicographers aren't so concerned about such niceties. In some cases, several variations of a given quote are floating around, and I've tried to pick the one that seems most reliable. (But remember what Hesketh Pearson said: "Misquotations are the only quotations that are never misquoted." Or something like that.)

Anyway, for any omissions and/or inaccuracies, I apologize in advance — though I make no apology for the several times that I've shamelessly quoted from my own books. After all, if *I* won't quote me, who will?

DWB,
Toronto, 1998

ACCORDION

A gentleman is a man who can play the accordion but doesn't.

— Anon.

Accordion, n. An instrument in harmony with the sentiments of an assassin.

— Ambrose Bierce (1842-1914),
American journalist, *The Devil's Dictionary* (1906).

ADVICE

When a piece gets difficult, make faces.

— Artur Schnabel (1882-1951),
Austrian pianist, giving advice
to fellow pianist Vladimir Horowitz.

We are here and it is now. Further than that all human knowledge is moonshine.

— H.L. Mencken (1880-1956),
American journalist and music critic.

1

In case of emergency:
1. Grab your coat.
2. Take your hat.
3. Leave your worries on the doorstep.
4. Direct your feet to the sunny side of the street.
— **Anon.**

Nature has given us two ears but only one mouth.
— **Benjamin Disraeli** (1804-81),
British prime minister.

Never compose anything unless not composing it becomes a positive nuisance to you.
— **Gustav Holst** (1874-1934),
British composer.

"To be played with both hands in the pocket."
— **Erik Satie** (1866-1925),
French composer, giving instructions
for one of his piano pieces.

Consort not with a female musician lest thou be taken in by her snares.
— **Ben Sira**,
The Book of Wisdom (ca. 190 BC).

Music hath charms to soothe the savage beast, but I'd try a revolver first.
— **Josh Billings** (1818-85),
American humorist.

If thine enemy offend thee, give his child a drum.
> — **Anon**.

Don't do unto others as you would have them do unto you — their tastes may be different.
> — **George Bernard Shaw** (1856-1950),
> Irish playwright and music critic.

Never hold discussions with the monkey when the organ grinder is in the room.
> — **Sir Winston Churchill** (1874-1965),
> British prime minister.

AGE

O! sir, I must not tell my age. They say women and music should never be dated.
> — **Oliver Goldsmith** (1730-1774),
> Irish writer, in *She Stoops to Conquer* (1773).

AMATEURS

Hell is full of musical amateurs. Music is the brandy of the damned.
> — **George Bernard Shaw** (1856-1950),
> Irish playwright and music critic, in *Man and Superman*.

Said Oscar Wilde: 'Each man kills the thing he loves.' For example, the amateur musician.

— **H.L. Mencken** (1880-1956),
American journalist and music critic.

The Artistic Temperament is a disease that afflicts amateurs.

— **G.K. Chesterton** (1874-1936),
British essayist, novelist and theologian.

AMERICAN MUSIC

The way to write American music is simple. All you have to do is be an American and then write any kind of music you wish.

— **Virgil Thompson** (1896-1989),
American composer and music critic.

ARCHITECTURE

Architecture, said Hegel, is frozen music. Donald Swann's music has been compared with defrosted architecture.

— **Michael Flanders** (1922-75),
British humorist and songwriter (with Donald Swann).

Writing about art is like dancing about architecture.

— **Anon**.

ART AND ARTISTS

All the arts in America are a gigantic racket run by unscrupulous men for unhealthy women.
> — **Sir Thomas Beecham** (1879-1961),
> British conductor, in the *London Observer* (May 5, 1946).

Art is a collaboration between God and the artist, and the less the artist does the better.
> — **André Gide** (1869-1951),
> French novelist.

ASTAIRE, FRED

Can't act. Can't sing. Balding. Can dance a little.
> — *MGM* summary of singer/dancer
> Fred Astaire's first screen test.

AUDIENCE PARTICIPATION

Together we should sing it,
It's just a children's song.
And if you do not know the words
— You'd better learn them!
> — **Peter, Paul and Mary**,
> American folk music trio, in a concert version of
> *Puff, The Magic Dragon.*

If you feel like singing along, don't.
> — **James Taylor** (b. 1948),
> American pop singer/songwriter, to an audience.

AUDIENCES

I know two kinds of audience only — one coughing and one not coughing.
> — **Artur Schnabel** (1882-1951),
> Austrian pianist, in *My Life and Music* (1961).

Will people in the cheaper seats clap your hands? All the rest of you, if you'll just rattle your jewelry ...
> — **John Lennon** (1940-80),
> British rock singer/songwriter,
> at a Royal Command Performance of The Beatles (1963).

Hell is a half-filled auditorium.
> — **Robert Frost** (1874-1963),
> American poet.

That reminds me, I'm playing a concert tonight.
> — **Fritz Kreisler** (1875-1962),
> Austrian violinist, on seeing a row of fish at the market.

Flint must be an extremely wealthy town: I see that each of you bought two or three seats.
> — **Victor Borge** (b. 1909),
> Danish-born American musical humorist,
> speaking to a half-full house in Flint, Michigan.

I do not believe in the collective wisdom of individual ignorance.
> — **Thomas Carlyle** (1795-1881)
> Scottish historian and writer.

Not content to have the audience in the palm of his hand, he goes one further and clenches his fist.
> — **Kenneth Tynan** (1927-1980),
> British theatre critic and producer, on singer Frankie Laine.

Furtwangler was once told in Berlin that the people in the back seats were complaining that they could not hear some of his soft passages. "It does not matter," he said, "they do not pay so much."
> — **Neville Cardus**,
> British music critic, in *The Manchester Guardian* (1935).

7

The audience strummed their cattarhs.
> — **Alexander Woollcott** (1887-1943),
> American journalist and critic.

AUDITIONS

It was the kind of show where the girls were are not auditioned — just measured.
> — **Irene Thomas** (b. 1920),
> British writer and broadcaster.

BACH, J.S.

You want something by Bach? Which one, Johann Sebastian or Jacques Offen?
> — **Victor Borge** (b. 1909),
> Danish-born American musical humorist.

Even Bach comes down to the basic suck, blow, suck, suck, blow.
> — **Larry Adler** (b. 1914),
> American-born British harmonica virtuoso.

There's no reason we can't be friends. We both play Bach. You in your way, I in his.
> — **Wanda Landawska** (1877-1959),
> Polish concert keyboardist, to a rival (attr.).

Bad Music

If one hears bad music, it is one's duty to drown it by one's conversation.
> — **Oscar Wilde** (1854-1900),
> Irish playwright and novelist,
> in *The Picture of Dorian Gray* (1891).

There is a lot of bad music in every age, and there is no reason why this one should be an exception.
> — **Harold C. Schonberg** (b. 1915),
> American music critic,
> in the *New York Times* (March 26, 1961).

Of course the music is a great difficulty. You see, if one plays good music, people don't listen, and if one plays bad music, people don't talk.
> — **Oscar Wilde** (1854-1900),
> Irish playwright and novelist.

There are more bad musicians than there is bad music.
> — **Isaac Stern** (b. 1920),
> Russian-born American violinist.

Extraordinary how potent cheap music is!
> — **Noel Coward** (1899-1973),
> British playwright and songwriter.

BAGPIPES

Others, when the bag-pipe sings i' the nose,
Cannot contain their urine.
— **William Shakespeare,** (1564-1616),
British playwright,
Shylock in *The Merchant of Venice* IV:1.

I understand the inventor of the bagpipes was inspired when he saw a man carrying an indignant, asthmatic pig under his arm. Unfortunately, the man-made sound never equalled the purity of the sound achieved by the pig.
— **Alfred Hitchcock** (1889-1980),
British film director.

BALLET

I don't understand anything about the ballet. All I know is that during the intervals the ballerinas stink like horses.
— **Anton Chekov** (1860-1904),
Russian playwright.

The regular and insatiable supporters of ballet are people too sluggish of intellect to listen to a play on the one hand, and too devoid of imagination to listen to fine music without accompanying action, on the other.
— **Alan Dent**,
drama critic of the *News Chronicle* (1952).

BANJO

I can see fiddling around with a banjo, but how do you banjo around with a fiddle?
— **Duncan Purney** (b. 1937),
American broadcaster, in *Musical Notes* (May 16, 1984).

BAROQUE MUSIC

Muzak for the intelligensia.
— **Anon.**,
on Baroque music, circa 1970.

BARTOK, BELA

He not only never wears his heart on his sleeve; he seems to have deposited it in some bank vault.
— **Colin Wilson** (b. 1931),
British novelist, on Bela Bartok,
in *Brandy of the Damned* (1964).

11

BEECHAM, SIR THOMAS

Hark! the herald angels sing!
Beecham's Pills are just the thing,
Two for a woman, one for a child,
Peace on earth and mercy mild!
> — **Sir Thomas Beecham** (1879-1961),
> British conductor.

At a rehearsal I let the orchestra play as they like.
At the concert I make them play as *I* like.
> — **Sir Thomas Beecham** (1879-1961),
> British conductor.

BEETHOVEN, LUDWIG VAN

If Beethoven had been killed in a plane crash at the age of 22, it would have changed the history of music — and of aviation.
> — **Tom Stoppard** (b. 1937),
> Czech-born British playwright.

I love Beethoven, especially the poems.
> — **Ringo Starr** (b. 1940),
> British rock drummer, The Beatles.

I occasionally play works by contemporary composers for two reasons. First to discourage the composer from writing any more and secondly to remind myself how much I appreciate Beethoven.

— **Jascha Heifetz** (1901-87),
Russian-born American violinist.

It is impossible to imagine Goethe or Beethoven being good at billiards or golf.

— **H.L. Mencken** (1880-1956),
American journalist and music critic.

Beethoven always sounds to me like the upsetting of a bag of nails, with here and there an also dropped hammer.

— **John Ruskin** (1819-1900),
British art critic and writer,
in a letter to John Brown (February 6, 1881).

Last night the band played Beethoven. Beethoven lost.

— **Anon**.

Beethoven's *Fifth Symphony* is the most sublime noise that has ever penetrated the ear of man.

— **E.M. Forster** (1879-1970),
British novelist, in *Howards End*.

BERLIOZ, HECTOR

Berlioz says nothing in his music, but he says it magnificently.

> — **James Gibbons Huneker** (1860-1921),
> American music critic and writer.

BERG, ALBAN

It is my private opinion that [Alban] Berg is just a bluff. But even if he isn't, it is impossible to deny that his music (?) is a soporiphic, by the side of which the telephone book is a strong cup of coffee.

> — **Samuel Chotzinoff**,
> in the *New York Post* (April 5, 1935).

BIOGRAPHY

My name is Hugo Wolf. I was born on March 13th 1860, and am still alive at the moment. That's biography enough.

> — **Hugo Wolf** (1860-1903),
> Austrian composer, replying to a request
> for biographical information.

BRAHMS, JOHANNES

If there is anyone here whom I have not insulted, I beg his pardon.
> — **Johannes Brahms** (1833-97),
> German composer, on leaving a party of friends.

Art is long and life is short: here is evidently the explanation of a Brahms symphony.
> — **Edward Lorne**,
> British writer, in *Fanfare*, London (January 1922).

[Brahms is] rather tiresomely addicted to dressing himself up as Handel or Beethoven and making a prolonged and intolerable noise.
> — **George Bernard Shaw** (1856-1950),
> Irish playwright and music critic,
> in *The World* (June 21, 1893).

BRAHMS REQUIEM

There are some experiences in life which should not be demanded twice from any man, and one of them is listening to the Brahms *Requiem*.
> — **George Bernard Shaw** (1856-1950),
> Irish playwright and music critic.

[The Brahms *Requiem*] is patiently borne only by the corpse.
> — **George Bernard Shaw** (1856-1950),
> Irish playwright and music critic.

Brahms's *Requiem* has not the true funeral relish: It is so execrably and ponderously dull that the very flattest of funerals would seem like a ballet, or at least a *danse macabre*, after it.
> — **George Bernard Shaw** (1856-1950),
> Irish playwright and music critic,
> in *The World* (November 9, 1892).

Brains

You don't need any brains to listen to music.
> — **Luciano Pavarotti** (b. 1935),
> Italian opera tenor (1994).

Brass

Brass bands are all very well in their place — outdoors and several miles away.
> — **Sir Thomas Beecham** (1879-1961),
> British conductor (attrib.).

CANON

Canon: ... Not to be confused with the ones required in the *1812 Overture*, which are spelt differently and which lack contrapuntal interest.

— **Anthony Hopkins**,
British music writer, in *Downbeat Music Guide* (1977).

CASTRATO

Eunuch: A man who has had his works cut out for him.

— **Robert Byrne**

[The castrato] represents what might be considered the ultimate example of putting art before common sense.
— **David W. Barber** (b. 1958),
Canadian journalist, humorist and musician,
When the Fat Lady Sings (1990).

CELLO

The cello is not one of my favorite instruments. It has such a lugubrious sound, like someone reading a will.
— **Irene Thomas** (b. 1920),
British writer and broadcaster.

Madame, there you sit with that magnificent instrument between your legs, and all you can do is *scratch* it!
— **Arturo Toscanini** (1867-1957),
Italian conductor, to a woman cellist.
Also attributed to Beecham.

CLASSICAL MUSIC

Classical music is music written by famous dead foreigners.

— **Arlene Heath**

Classical music is the kind we keep thinking will turn into a tune.
— **Frank McKinny (Kin) Hubbard** (1868-1930),
American journalist, *Comments of Abe Martin and His Neighbors* (1923).

COMMUNISM

Communism doesn't work because people like to own stuff.
— **Frank Zappa** (1941-1997),
American rock musician, Mothers of Invention.

COMPOSERS AND COMPOSING

Give me a laundry list and I'll set it to music.
— **Gioacchino Rossini** (1792-1868),
Italian composer.

The main thing the public demands of a composer is that he be dead.
— **Arthur Honneger** (1892-1955),
French composer, (when he was still alive).

The good composer is slowly discovered; the bad composer is slowly found out.
— **Ernest Newman** (1868-1959),
British music critic.

Composers shouldn't think too much — it interferes with their plagiarism.
— **Howard Dietz** (1896-1983),
American songwriter.

Before I compose a piece, I walk round it several times, accompanied by myself.

— **Erik Satie** (1866-1925),
French composer.

When I was young, people used to say to me: Wait until you're fifty, you'll see. I am fifty. I haven't seen anything.

— **Erik Satie** (1866-1925),
French composer.

You have to develop in many different directions, because composers are so useless.

— **John Beckwith** (b. 1927),
Canadian critic, essayist, educator and composer,
quoted in *The Globe and Mail* (January 10, 1998).

In order to compose, all you need to do is remember a tune that nobody else has thought of.

— **Robert Schumann** (1810-1856),
German composer.

Do *I* send you *my* works to look at?

— **Camille Saint-Saëns** (1835-1921),
French composer, returning unsolicited compositions.

CONDUCTORS AND CONDUCTING

I kissed my first girl and smoked my first cigarette on the same day. I haven't had time for tobacco since.
— **Arturo Toscanini** (1867-1957),
Italian conductor.

There's only one woman I know of who could never be a symphony conductor, and that's the Venus de Milo.
— **Margaret Hillis** (b. 1921),
American conductor.

There are two golden rules for an orchestra: start together and finish together. The public doesn't give a damn what goes on in between.
— **Sir Thomas Beecham** (1879-1961),
British conductor.

I am not the greatest conductor in this country. On the other hand, I'm better than any damned foreigner.
— **Sir Thomas Beecham** (1879-1961),
British conductor, in the *Daily Express* (March 9, 1961).

Why do we have to have all these third-rate foreign conductors around — when we have so many second-rate ones of our own?
— **Sir Thomas Beecham** (1879-1961),
British conductor.

They are for prima donnas or corpses — I am neither.
— **Arturo Toscanini** (1867-1957),
Italian conductor, refusing a wreath of flowers after a concert.

After I die, I shall return to Earth as a gatekeeper of a bordello and I won't let any of you — not a one of you — enter!
— **Arturo Toscanini** (1867-1957),
Italian conductor, to an orchestra.

Can't you read? The score demands *con amore*, and what are you doing? You are playing it like married men!
— **Arturo Toscanini** (1867-1957),
Italian conductor, to an orchestra.

This backward man, this view obstructor,
Is known to us as the conductor.
— **Lawrence McKinney**

We cannot expect you to be with us all the time, but perhaps you could be good enough to keep in touch now and again.

— **Sir Thomas Beecham** (1879-1961),
British conductor, during a rehearsal.

COUNTRY MUSIC

There's a lot of things blamed on me that never happened. But then, there's a lot of things that I did that I never got caught at.

— **Johnny Cash** (b. 1932),
American country singer/songwriter.

CREDO

The *Credo* is the longest movement. There is much to believe.

— **Igor Stravinsky** (1882-1971),
Russian-born American composer, commenting on his *Mass*.

CRITICS AND CRITICISM

A critic is a man who knows the way but can't drive the car.

— **Kenneth Tynan** (1927-1980),
British theatre critic and producer.

Critics are like eunuchs in a harem. They're there every night, they see it done every night, they see how it should be done every night, but they can't do it themselves.
— **Brendan Behan** (1923-64),
Irish playwright.

A critic is a legless man who teaches running.
— **Channing Pollock** (1880-1946).

I am sitting in the smallest room of my house. I have your review before me. In a moment it will be behind me.
— **Max Reger** (1873-1916),
German composer, responding to critic Rudof Louis (1906).

I cried all the way to the bank.
— **Liberace** (1919-87),
(Vladzin Valentino Liberace),
American pianist, on his reaction to criticism.

I had another dream the other day about music critics. They were small and rodent-like with padlocked ears, as if they had stepped out of a painting by Goya.
— **Igor Stravinsky** (1882-1971),
Russian-born American composer,
in *The Evening Standard* (October 29, 1969).

A statue has never been set up in honor of a critic.
— **Jean Sibelius** (1865-1957),
Finnish composer.

The trouble with music critics is that so often they have the score in their hands and not in their heads.
— **Sir Thomas Beecham** (1879-1961),
British conductor.

You know, the critics never change; I'm still getting the same notices I used to get as a child. They tell me I play very well for my age.
— **Mischa Elman** (1891-1967),
Russian-born American violinist, in his 70s.

Critics can't even make music by rubbing their back legs together.
— **Mel Brooks** (b. 1927),
American film director, writer and actor,
in *The New York Times* (1975).

Nature fits all her children with something to do,
He that would write and can't write can surely review.
— **James Russell Lowell** (1819-91),
American astronomer and writer, *A Fable for Critics*.

A critic is a necessary evil, and criticism is an evil necessity.
— **Carolyn Wells** (1869-1942),
American novelist.

[The critic] is forced to be literate about the illiterate, witty about the witless and coherent about the incoherent.

— **John Crosby**

A critic is a bunch of biases held loosely together by a sense of taste.

— **Witney Balliett**,
Dinosaurs in the Morning (1962).

When Frank Sinatra, Jr. was kidnapped, I said "It must have been done by music critics."

— **Oscar Levant** (1906-72),
American film actor, composer and pianist,
Memoirs of an Amnesiac.

The lot of critics is to be remembered for what they failed to understand.

— **George Moore**

I paid a shilling for my programme. The editor informs me with the law of libel in its present unsatisfactory condition, I must not call this a fraud, a cheat, a swindle, an imposition, an exorbitance, or even an overcharge.

> — **George Bernard Shaw** (1856-1950),
> Irish playwright and music critic.

Last year, I gave several lectures on 'Intelligence and Musicality in Animals.' Today, I shall speak to you about 'Intelligence and Musicality in Critics.' The subject is very similar.

> — **Erik Satie** (1866-1925),
> French composer, in a lecture *In Praise of Critics* (1918).

Never speak ill of yourself; your friends will always say enough on that subject.

> — **Charles M. de Talleyrand-Périgord** (1754-1838),
> French statesman.

Pornophony.

> — **Anon.**, American critic,
> on Shostakovich's opera *Lady Macbeth of Mtensk*.

Criticism of our contemporaries is not criticism; it is conversation.

> — **Jules Lamaître**

I can take any amount of criticism, so long as it is unqualified praise.

— **Noel Coward** (1899-1973),
British playwright and songwriter.

Honest criticism is hard to take, particularly from a relative, a friend, an acquaintance or a stranger.

— **Franklin P. Jones**

If a literary man puts together two words about music, one of them will be wrong.

— **Aaron Copland** (1900-90),
American composer.

The audience came out whistling the set.

— **Anon**. American critic,
on Irving Berlin's *Miss Liberty* (1949).

Assassination is the extreme form of censorship.

— **George Bernard Shaw** (1856-1950),
Irish playwright and music critic.

The music of *The Love for Three Oranges*, I fear, is too much for this generation. After intensive study and close observation at rehearsal and performance, I detected the beginnings of two tunes.

— **Edward Moore**,
Chicago Tribune (December 31, 1921).

It sounds as if someone had smeared the score of *Tristan* while it was still wet.

— **Anon**. contemporary,
on Schöenberg's *Verklärte Nacht*.

Remember that nobody will ever get ahead of you as long as he is kicking you in the seat of the pants.

Walter Winchell (1879-1972),
American journalist.

I found myself referring to the programme to find out whether I ought to be seeing red or looking blue at certain moments, and some of it made many of the audience feel green.

— *The London Times*,
reviewing Arthur Bliss's *A Colour Symphony* (1922).

Don't pay any attention to the critics — don't even ignore them.

— **Samuel Goldwyn** (1882-1974),
Polish-born American film producer.

Having the critics praise you is like having the hangman say you've got a pretty neck.

— **Eli Wallach** (b. 1915),
American film actor.

CROSBY, BING

There is nothing in the world I wouldn't do for [Bob] Hope, and there is nothing he wouldn't do for me. ... We spend our days doing nothing for each other.

— **Bing Crosby** (1904-77),
American singer and film actor,
in *The Observer* (May 7, 1950).

Oh, the kinda singing I do, you can't hurt your voice.

— **Bing Crosby** (1904-77),
American singer and film actor.

CULTURE

When I hear the word 'culture' I reach for my gun.

— **Hanns Johst** (b. 1890) (circa 1939),
also attributed to Nazi officer Herman Goering.

Culture is what your butcher would have if he were a surgeon.

— **Mary Pettibone Poole**

Intellectuals should never marry; they might enjoy it; and besides, they should not reproduce themselves.

— **Don Herold**

DANCERS AND DANCING

The trouble with nude dancing is that not everything stops when the music stops.
— **Sir Robert Helpmann** (1909-86),
Australian dancer/choreographer,
on the nude musical *Oh, Calcutta!*

DEBUSSY, CLAUDE

I have already heard it. I had better not go: I will start to get accustomed to it and finally like it.
— **Nikolai Rimsky-Korsakov** (1844-1908),
Russian composer, on a concert of Debussy's music.

Delius, Frederick

The musical equivalent of blancmange.
>— **Bernard Levin** (b. 1928),
> British writer and critic, of Frederick Delius (1983).

Disco

Disco dancing is ... just the steady thump of a giant moron knocking in an endless nail.
>— **Clive James** (b. 1939),
> Australian-born British journalist and critic, in the London
> *Sunday Observer* (December 17, 1978).

DJs

I am amazed at radio DJs today. I am firmly convinced that AM on my radio stands for Absolute Moron. I will not begin to tell you what FM stands for.
>— **Jasper Carrott** (b. 1942),
> British comic.

Death

It is impossible to experience one's death objectively and still carry a tune.
>— **Woody Allen** (b. 1935),
> American comic and filmmaker.

Ear

Because I have no ear for music, at the concert of the Quintette Club, it looked to me as if the performers were crazy, and all the audience were make-believe crazy, in order to soothe the lunatics and keep them amused.

— **Ralph Waldo Emerson** (1803-82),
American poet and writer, *Journals*.

He has Van Gogh's ear for music.

— **Billy Wilder** (b. 1906),
Austrian-born American film director, on actor Clift Osmond.

Elgar, Edward

Holy water in a German beer barrel.

— **George Moore**,
on Elgar's *Dream of Gerontius*.

Fiddle

Perhaps it was because Nero played the fiddle, they burned Rome.

— **Oliver Herford** (1863-1935),
British-born American humorist.

He was a fiddler, and consequently a rogue.
>— **Jonathan Swift** (1667-1745),
>Irish writer and clergyman.

FILM MUSIC

A [film] musician is like a mortician. He can't bring a body to life, but he can make it look better.
>— **Adolf Deutsch** (1898-1980),
>American film composer.

FLUTE

Of all musicians, flautists are most obviously the ones who know something we don't know.
>— **Paul Jennings** (b. 1918),
>British humorist, *Flautists Flaunt Afflatus*,
>*The Jenguin Pennings*.

FOLK MUSIC

The farmer's daughter hath soft brown hair
(Butter and eggs and a pound of cheese);
And I met a ballad, I can't say where
Which wholly consisted of lines like these.
>— **C.S. Calverley** (1831-84),
>British poet, *Ballad*.

The only thing to do with a folk melody, once you have played it, is to play it louder.

— **Anon**.

A folksinger is someone who sings through his nose by ear.

— **Anon**.

If I had a hammer, I'd use it on Peter, Paul, and Mary.
— **Howard Rosenberg**

FUNERAL MUSIC

Very nice, but tell me frankly, don't you think it would have been better if it had been *you* who had died, and your *uncle* who had written the *Funeral March*?
— attributed to **Gioacchino Rossini** (1792-1868), Italian composer, on being shown funeral music for Giacomo Meyerbeer (1791-1864), composed by Meyerbeer's nephew.

GERSHWIN, GEORGE

The European boys have small ideas but they sure know how to dress 'em up.
— **George Gershwin** (1898-1937), American composer, on the music of Arthur Honneger.

GOD

Why attack God? He may be as miserable as we are.
— **Erik Satie** (1866-1925),
French composer.

God tells me how the music should sound, but you stand in the way!
— **Arturo Toscanini** (1867-1957),
Italian conductor, reprimanding a trumpet player.

The German imagines even God is a singer.
— **Friedrich Nietszche** (1844-1900),
German philosoper.

GOLDBERG VARIATIONS

I don't know much about classical music. For years I thought the *Goldberg Variations* were something Mr. and Mrs. Goldberg tried on their wedding night.
> — **Woody Allen** (b. 1935),
> American comic and filmmaker,
> in *Stardust Memories* (1980).

HARP

Harpists spend 90 per cent of their lives tuning their harps and 10 per cent playing out of tune.
> — **Igor Stravinsky** (1882-1971),
> Russian-born American composer.

HARPSICHORD

The sound of the harpsichord resembles that of a bird-cage played with a toasting-fork.
> — **Sir Thomas Beecham** (1879-1961),
> British conductor.

A scratch with a sound at the end of it.
> — **Anon.**,
> quoted by Percy A. Scholes (1877-1958),
> in *The Oxford Companion to Music*.

37

Two skeletons copulating on a corrugated tin roof.
— **Sir Thomas Beecham** (1879-1961),
British conductor.

Haydn, Franz Joseph

Haydn had neither the flashy individuality of Mozart nor the brooding, romantic passion of Beethoven. He was more of a middle-management type.
— **David W. Barber** (b. 1958),
Canadian journalist, humorist and musician,
Bach, Beethoven and the Boys (1986).

Hearing

To listen is an effort, and just to hear is no merit. A duck hears also.
— **Igor Stravinsky** (1822-1971),
Russian-born American composer.

INSPIRATION

All the inspiration I ever needed was a phone call from a producer.

> — **Cole Porter** (1893-1964),
> American songwriter.

Nothing primes inspiration more than necessity, whether it be the presence of a copyist waiting for your work, or the prodding of an impresario tearing his hair. In my time, all the impresarios of Italy were bald at thirty.

> — **Gioacchino Rossini** (1792-1868),
> Italian composer.

INSULTS

No one can have a higher opinion of him than I have, and I think he's a dirty little beast.

> — **W. S. Gilbert** (1836-1911),
> British operetta librettist.

Every time I look at you I get a fierce desire to be lonesome.

> — **Oscar Levant** (1906-72),
> American film actor, composer and pianist.

Jazz

Madam, if you don't know by now, DON'T MESS WITH IT!

> — **Fats Waller** (1904-43),
> American jazz pianist, asked to define jazz.

If you see me up there on the stand smiling, I'm lost!
> — **Earl "Fatha" Hines** (b. 1905),
> American jazz musician.

A jazz musician is a juggler who uses harmonies instead of oranges.

> — **Benny Green** (b. 1923),
> American jazz trombonist, *The Reluctant Art* (1962).

Man, I can't *listen* that fast.
> — **Unnamed jazz musician**,
> on hearing Charlie Parker and Dizzie Gillespie's *Shaw Nuff*.

Playing 'bop' is like playing Scrabble with all the vowels missing.
> — **Duke Ellington** (1899-1974),
> American jazz musician, in *Look* magazine (August 10, 1954).

I'll play it first and tell you what it is later.
> — **Miles Davis** (1926-1991),
> American jazz trumpeter and composer.

That's just like tapping a nightingale on the shoulder, saying 'How's that again, dickey-bird?'
> — **Louis Armstrong** (1898-1971),
> American jazz trumpeter, to Danny Kaye (1913-87),
> on why nobody writes down Dixieland,
> in *The Five Pennies* (1959).

Epitaph for a tombstone of a cool musician: "Man, this cat is really gone."
> — *More Playboy's Party Jokes* (1965).

LIFE

Life is what happens to you while you're busy making other plans.
> — **John Lennon** (1940-80),
> British singer/songwriter, The Beatles.

Hey, if my life were easy, *anyone* could do it.
> — **David W. Barber** (b. 1958),
> Canadian journalist, humorist and musician.

LISZT, FRANZ

I know his mother only by correspondence, and one cannot arrange that sort of thing by correspondence.
> — **Franz Liszt** (1811-86),
> Hungarian pianist, on rumors that he
> fathered pianist Franz Servais.

LLOYD WEBBER, SIR ANDREW

Lloyd Webber's music is everywhere, but so is AIDS.
— **Malcolm Williamson** (b. 1931),
Australian music director to Queen Elizabeth II.

A confusing jamboree of piercing noise, routine roller-skating, misogyny and Orwellian special effects, *Starlight Express* is the perfect gift for the kid who has everything except parents.

— **Frank Rich**,
New York Times, reviewing
the Andrew Lloyd Webber musical.

LOVE

Love is not the dying moan of a distant violin — it's the triumphant twang of a bedspring.
— **S.J. Perelman** (1904-79),
American humorist.

What the world really needs is more love and less paperwork.

— **Pearl Bailey** (1918-90),
American jazz singer.

I sigh, I pine,
I squeak, I squawk.
Today I woke
too weak to walk.

> — **Stephen Sondheim** (b. 1930),
> American lyricist and composer,
> in *A Funny Thing Happened on the Way to the Forum.*

MADONNA

[Madonna is] like a breast with a boom box.

> — **Judy Tenuta**,
> American comedian.

Madonna shaved her legs to lose 30 pounds.

> — **Joan Rivers**,
> American comedian.

Michael keeps asking why I can't write songs like Madonna. I tell him because I have brains.

> — **Cristina**,
> British pop singer.

Madonna and Sean Penn — beauty and the beast, but guess which one?

> — **Joan Rivers**,
> American comedian.

MCCARTNEY, SIR PAUL

Paul McCartney ... has become the oldest living cute boy in the world.
— **Anna Quindlen**,
in *The New York Times.*

MELODY

Melody! The battle-cry of *dilettanti*!
— **Robert Schumann** (1810-56),
German composer.

MESSIAH

I should be sorry, my Lord, if I had only succeeded in entertaining them; I wished to make them better.
— **G.F. Handel** (1685-1759),
German-born British composer, to Lord Kinnoull, after the first
London performance of *Messiah* (March 23, 1743).

Just a little more reverence, please, and not so much astonishment.
— **Sir Malcolm Sargent** (1895-1967),
British conductor, rehearsing a female chorus in *For Unto Us
a Child is Born*, from Handel's *Messiah.*

Come for tea. Come for tea, my people.

> — **Anon.**,
> parodying the opening tenor aria of Handel's *Messiah*.

Military Music

Military justice is to justice what military music is to music.

> — **Groucho Marx** (1890-1977),
> American comedic film star.

Mistakes

When a musician hath forgot his note,
He makes as though a crumb
stuck in his throat.

> — **John Clarke**,
> *Paroemiologia* (1639).

Modern Music

I don't write modern music. I only write good music.

> — **Igor Stravinsky** (1882-1971),
> Russian-born American composer.

Three farts and a raspberry, orchestrated.
— **Sir John Barbirolli** (1899-1970),
British conductor, describing modern music.

My music is not modern, it is only badly played.
— **Arnold Schoenberg** (1874-1951),
Austrian-born American composer.

That's the worst of my reputation as a modern composer — everyone must have thought I meant it.
— **Igor Stravinsky** (1882-1971),
Russian-born American composer,
on a misprint in one of his scores.

MOZART, WOLFGANG AMADEUS

Mozart is just God's way of making the rest of us feel insignificant.
— **David W. Barber** (b. 1958),
Canadian journalist, humorist and musician,
Bach, Beethoven and the Boys (1986).

Ah, Mozart! He was happily married — but his wife wasn't.

> — **Victor Borge** (b. 1909),
> Danish-born American musical humorist.

I write as a sow piddles.

> — **Wolfgang Amadeus Mozart** (1719-87),
> Austrian composer, in a letter.

Nothing from Mozart?

> — **Sir Thomas Beecham** (1879-1961),
> British conductor, on hearing his 70th birthday telegrams.

The *G-minor Symphony* consists of eight remarkable measures ... surrounded by a half-hour of banality.

> — **Glenn Gould** (1930-1980),
> Canadian pianist and broadcaster,
> on Mozart's *Symphony No. 40*,
> in *The Glenn Gould Reader* (1984).

It's people like that who make you realize how little you've accomplished. It is a sobering thought, for example, that when Mozart was my age — he had been dead for two years!

> — **Tom Lehrer** (b. 1928),
> American musical satirist, on Alma Mahler Gropius Werfel.

MTV

MTV is the lava lamp of the 1980s.

— **Doug Ferrari**

When I was young we didn't have MTV. We had to take drugs and go to concerts.

— **Steven Pearl**

MURRAY, ANNE

If you close your eyes and think of a naked Anne Murray, parts of her always come up airbrushed.

— **Larry LeBlanc** (b. 1950),
on the wholesome Canadian country-pop songbird,
in *Maclean's* magazine (November 1974).

MUSIC AND MUSICIANS

These three take crooked ways: carts, boats and musicians.

— **Hindu proverb**

Only sick music makes money today.

— **Friedrich Nietzsche** (1844-1900),
German philosopher, (in 1888).

Music is essentially useless, as is life.
> — **George Santayana** (1863-1952),
> Spanish-born American philosopher.

Music is but a fart that's sent
From the guts of an instrument.
> — **Anon.**,
> *Wit and Drollery* (1645).

Too many pieces [of music] finish too long after the end.
> — **Igor Stravinsky** (1882-1971),
> Russian-born American composer.

Music with dinner is an insult both to the cook and the violinist.
> — **G.K. Chesterton** (1874-1936),
> British essayist, novelist and theologian.

The English may not like music — but they absolutely love the noise it makes.
> — **Sir Thomas Beecham** (1879-1961),
> British conductor, in the *New York Herald Tribune*
> (March 9, 1961).

My music is best understood by children and animals.
> — **Igor Stravinsky** (1882-1971),
> Russian-born American composer.

Nothing is more odious than music without hidden meaning.

> — **Frédéric Chopin** (1810-49),
> Polish-born French composer, in *La Courier musical* (1910).

"I know I have to beat time when I learn music."
"Ah! That accounts for it," said the Hatter. "He won't stand beating."

> — **Lewis Carroll** (1832-1898),
> British writer, in *Alice's Adventures in Wonderland* (1865).

"This *must* be music," said he,"of the *spears*,
For I am cursed if each note of it doesn't run through one!"

> — **Thomas Moore** (1779-1852),
> Irish poet, in *The Fudge Family in Paris*.

We often feel sad in the presence of music without words; and often more than that in the presence of music without music.

> — **Mark Twain** (1835-1910),
> American journalist and humorist.

Music is another lady that talks charmingly and says nothing.

> — **Austin O'Malley**

I hate music, especially when it's played.

> — **Jimmy Durante** (1893-1980),
> American entertainer/comedian.

When you are about 35 years old, something terrible happens to music.

— **Steve Race**,
BBC Radio disk-jockey (1982).

MUSIC HALL

The other evening, feeling rather in want of a headache, I bethought me that I had not been to a music hall for a long time.

— **George Bernard Shaw** (1856-1950),
Irish playwright and music critic.

MUSICALS

I want to do a musical movie. Like *Evita*, but with good music.

— **Sir Elton John** (b. 1947),
British singer/songwriter (1996).

The hills are alive — and it's rather frightening!
> — **Anon**., parodying Rodgers and
> Hammerstein's *The Sound of Music*.

It doesn't stand up to huge intellectual scrutiny.
> — **Sir Andrew Lloyd Webber** (b. 1948),
> British composer, on his musical *Phantom of the Opera*.

MUSICOLOGY

A musicologist is a man who can read music but can't hear it.
> — **Sir Thomas Beecham** (1879-1961),
> British conductor.

MUZAK

Muzak goes in one ear and out some other opening.
> — **Anton Kuerti** (b. 1938),
> Austrian-born Canadian pianist,
> in Ulla Colgrass, *For the Love of Music* (1988).

I worry that the person who thought up Muzak may be thinking up something else.
> — **Lily Tomlin** (b. 1939),
> American comic.

NOISE

Of all noises, I think music is the least disagreeable.
— **Samuel Johnson** (1709-84),
British lexicographer and diarist.

NONSENSE

Nothing is capable of being well set to music that is not nonsense.
— **Joseph Addison** (1672-1719),
British essayist, in *The Spectator* (1711).

OPERA

Bed is the poor man's opera.

— **Italian proverb**

I do not mind what language an opera is sung in so long as it is a language I don't understand.
— **Edward Appleton** (1892-1965),
British physicist.

No good opera plot can be sensible, for people do not sing when they are feeling sensible.
—**W.H. Auden** (1907-73),
British poet.

Opera in English is, in the main, just about as sensible as baseball in Italian.
> — **H.L. Mencken** (1880-1956),
> American journalist and music critic.

You can't judge Egypt by *Aïda*.
> — **Ronald Firbank** (1886-1926),
> British novelist.

I liked your opera. I think I will set it to music.
> — **Ludwig van Beethoven** (1770-1827),
> German composer, to fellow composer Ferdinando Paër,
> on his opera *Leonore*.

Opera's when a guy gets stabbed in the back and instead of bleeding he sings.
> — **Ed Gardner** (1905-1963),
> *Duffy's Tavern*.

[Opera is] an exotic and irrational entertainment.
> — **Samuel Johnson** (1709-84),
> British lexicographer and diarist.

An opera, like a pillory, may be said
To nail our ears down, and expose our head.
> — **Edward Young** (1683-1765),
> British poet, *Satires*.

Do it big or stay in bed.
> — **Larry Kelly**,
> American opera producer.

Going to the Opera, like getting drunk, is a sin that carries its own punishment with it, and that a very severe one.
> — **Hannah More** (1745-1833),
> letter to her sister.

How wonderful opera would be if there were no singers.
> — **Gioacchino Rossini** (1792-1868),
> Italian composer (of operas).

Nobody really sings in an opera — they just make loud noises.
> — **Amelita Galli-Curci** (1882-1963),
> Italian operatic soprano.

[Opera is] the most rococo and degraded of all art forms.
> — **William Morris** (1834-1896),
> British designer, artist and poet.

I wholly agree with Arnold Bennett, who maintained that an opera was tolerable only when sung in a language he didn't understand.
> — **James Agate** (1877-1947),
> British theatre critic (1945).

Like German opera, too long and too loud.
> — **Evelyn Waugh** (1903-66),
> British novelist, describing the Battle of Crete (1941).

I sometimes wonder which would be nicer — an opera without an interval, or an interval without an opera.
> — **Ernest Newman** (1869-1959),
> British music critic and writer.

People are wrong when they say the opera isn't what it used to be. It *is* what it used to be. That's what's wrong with it.
> — **Noel Coward** (1899-1973),
> British playwright and songwriter, *Design for Living*.

An unalterable and unquestioned law of the musical world required that German text of French operas sung by Swedish artists should be translated into Italian for the clearer understanding of English-speaking audiences.
> — **Edith Wharton** (1863-1937),
> American novelist, in *The Age of Innocence*.

I would rather sing grand opera than listen to it.
> — **Don Herold**

I liked the opera very much. Everything but the music.
> — British composer **Benjamin Britten** (1913-76),
> to British poet **W.H. Auden** (1907-73),
> on hearing Stravinsky's *The Rake's Progress*.

The opera ... is to music what a bawdy house is to a cathedral.

> — **H.L. Mencken** (1880-1956),
> American journalist and music critic.

Sleep is an excellent way of listening to an opera.

> — **James Stephens**

The opera is like a husband with a foreign title: expensive to support, hard to understand and therefore a supreme social challenge.

> — **Cleveland Armory**,
> British writer and critic.

The first act of the three occupied three hours, and I enjoyed that in spite of the singing.

> — **Mark Twain** (1835-1910),
> American journalist and humourist,
> in *A Tramp Abroad* (1880).

It was pretty good. Even the music was nice.

> — **Yogi Berra** (b. 1925),
> American baseball player, after attending an opera.

ORCHESTRA

A piece for orchestra without music.

> — **Maurice Ravel** (1875-1937),
> French composer, on his piece *Bolero*.

Overtures

I tried to resist his overtures, but he plied me with symphonies, quartets, chamber music and cantatas.
— **S.J. Perelman** (1904-79),
American jouralist and humorist.

Paganini, Niccola

I have wept only three times in my life: the first time when my earliest opera failed, the second time when, with a boating party, a truffled turkey fell into the water, and the third time when I first heard Paganini play.
— **Gioacchino Rossini** (1792-1868),
Italian composer.

Phonograph

Phonograph: n. An irritating toy that restores life to dead noises.
— **Ambrose Bierce** (1842-1914),
American journalist,
The Devil's Dictionary (1906).

PIANO

Piano. n. A parlor utensil for subduing the impenitent visitor. It is operated by depressing the keys of the machine and the spirits of the audience.

— **Ambrose Bierce** (1842-1914),
American journalist,
The Devil's Dictionary (1906).

I wish the Government would put a tax on pianos for the incompetent.

— **Edith Sitwell** (1887-1964),
British writer.

I always make sure that the lid over the keyboard is open before I start to play.

— **Artur Schnabel** (1882-1951),
Austrian pianist, asked the secret of piano playing.

Nothing soothes me more after a long and maddening course of pianoforte recitals than to sit and have my teeth drilled.

— **George Bernard Shaw** (1856-1950),
Irish playwright and music critic.

Don't tell my mother I'm in politics — she thinks I play piano in a whorehouse.

— **Anon**.

It is said about [Henry] Cowell that he has invented tonal groups that can be played on the piano with the aid of fists and forearms! Why so coy? With one's behind one can cover many more notes!

— **Paul Zschorlich**,
Deutsche Zeitung, Berlin (March 13, 1932).

When she started to play, Steinway himself came down personally and rubbed his name off the piano.

— **Bob Hope** (b. 1903),
American comedian, on comedian Phyllis Diller.

PIPER

Give the piper a penny to play, and twopence to leave off.

— **Thomas Fuller** (1654-1734),
British poet, *Gnomologia* (1732).

He must be a poor sort of man, for otherwise he would not be so good a piper.
— **Antisthenes** (c. 450-380 BCE),
Greek philosopher.

PLAGIARISM

It's much too good for him. He did not know what to do with it.
— **G.F. Handel** (1685-1759),
German-born British composer, on using material composed by his rival Bononcini.

Immature artists imitate. Mature artists steal.
— **Lionel Trilling** (1905-75),
American writer.

A good composer does not imitate; he steals.
— **Igor Stravinsky** (1882-1971),
Russian-born American composer.

Remember why the good Lord made your eyes — plagiarize!
— **Tom Lehrer** (b. 1928),
American songwriter and satirist.

PRACTISING

If I don't practice one day, I know it; two days, the critics know it; three days, the public knows it.
— **Jascha Heifetz** (1901-87),
Russian-born American violinist,
in the *San Francisco Examiner* (April 18, 1971).

I never practise, I always play.
— **Wanda Landawska** (1877-1959),
Polish concert keyboardist.

RAVEL, MAURICE

Who can unravel Ravel?
— **Louis Elson**,
Boston *Daily Advertiser* (December 27, 1913).

Although Ravel's official biography does not mention it, I feel sure that at the age of three he swallowed a musical snuff-box, and at nine he must have been frightened by a bear. To both phenomena he offers repeated testimony: he is constantly tinkling high on the harps and celesta, or is growling low in the bassoons and double-basses.
— **Edward Robinson**,
The American Mercury, New York (May, 1932).

REPERTOIRE

I do not see any good reason why the devil should have all the good tunes.
— **Rowland Hill** (1744-1833),
British clergyman.

I know only two tunes: one of them is *Yankee Doodle* and the other one isn't.
— **Ulysses S. Grant** (1822-1885),
American Civil War general.

REGER, MAX

Reger might be epitomized as a composer whose name is the same either forward or backward, and whose music, curiously, often displays the same characteristic.
— **Irving Kolodin**,
New York Sun (November 14, 1934).

RELIGIOUS MUSIC

I didn't know *Onward, Christian Soldiers* was a Christian song.
— **Aggie Pate**,
at a non-denominational
mayor's breakfast in Fort Worth, Texas.

Rimsky-Korsakov, Nikolai

Rimsky-Korsakov — what a name! It suggests fierce whiskers stained with vodka!

> — *Musical Courier*,
> New York (October 27, 1897).

Rock and Pop Music

I don't know anything about music. In my line you don't have to.

> — **Elvis Presley** (1935-77),
> American pop singer.

Most rock journalism is people who cannot write interviewing people who cannot talk.

> — **Frank Zappa** (1940-1997),
> American rock musician, Mothers of Invention.

The typical rock fan is not smart enough to know when he is being dumped on.

> — **Frank Zappa** (1940-1997),
> American rock musician, Mothers of Invention.

Boy George is all England needs — another queen who can't dress.

> — **Joan Rivers**,
> American comedian.

It's one thing to want to save lives in Ethiopia, but it's another thing to inflict so much torture on the British public.
— **Morrissey (Steven Patrick)** (b. 1959),
Rock singer/songwriter, on the *Band Aid* concert.

If white bread could sing, it would sound like Olivia Newton-John.
— **Anon**.

It's all right letting yourself go, as long as you can let yourself back.
— **Mick Jagger** (b. 1943),
British singer/songwriter, The Rolling Stones.

The popular music industry has tried, repeatedly, to do with music what Ford attempts with cars. It works better with cars.
— **Tony Palmer** (b. 1941),
British music writer, in *All You Need is Love* (1976).

I've always said that pop music is disposable. ... If it wasn't disposable, it'd be a pain in the fuckin' arse.
— **Sir Elton John** (b. 1947),
British singer/songwriter.

They look like boys whom any self-respecting mum would lock in the bathroom.
— **The *London Daily Express***,
on The Rolling Stones (1964).

When I first started playing guitar, you didn't play gigs so much as just went out and tested your gear.

> — **Jeff Beck** (b. 1944),
> British rock guitarist.

If Patty Hearst were on *United Artists Records*, she never would have been found.

> — **Dean Torrence**

The image we have would be hard for Mickey Mouse to maintain.

> — **Karen Carpenter** (1950-1983),
> American pop singer, The Carpenters.

We're Pat Boone, only cleaner.

> — **Richard Carpenter** (b. 1945),
> Karen's brother.

My persona is so confused it even confuses me.
— **David Bowie** (b. 1947),
British singer/songwriter.

People take us far too seriously. We're going to have to start being far more stupid.
— **David Byrne** (b. 1952),
Scottish-born American singer/songwriter, Talking Heads.

I don't think anybody ever made it with a girl because they had a Tom Waits album on their shelves. I've got all three, and it never helped me.
— **Tom Waits** (b. 1949),
American singer/songwriter.

The only trouble with going to Heaven is that I'm scared there's no nightclubs there.
— **Tom Waits** (b. 1949),
American singer/songwriter.

Reporting I'm drunk is like saying there was a Tuesday last week.
— **Grace Slick** (b. 1943),
American rock singer,
Jefferson Airplane.

I don't expect *Short People* to be a big commercial success in Japan.
— **Randy Newman** (b. 1943),
American singer/songwriter.

We wanted to see America. It wasn't entirely successful. I kept falling asleep. It was a long drive.
— **Mick Jones** (b. 1955),
British rock musician, on a tour with The Clash.

Suppose they gave a war and no one came?
— **Arlo Guthrie** (1947-1967),
American folksinger/songwriter.

I'm going to run for President and when I get elected I'll assassinate myself. That'll set a precedent.
— **Spencer Dryden** (b. 1943),
American rock musician, Jefferson Airplane.

I manage to look so young because I'm mentally retarded.
— **Debbie Harry** (b. 1945),
American pop singer, Blondie.

We would rather be rich than famous. That is, more rich and slightly less famous.
— **John Lennon** (1940-80),
British rock singer/songwriter, The Beatles.

I'm the man who put the unk into the funk.
— **Muddy Waters** (1914-83),
American blues musician.

I never considered myself the greatest, but I am the best.

> — **Jerry Lee Lewis** (b. 1935),
> American rock musician.

The Rolling Stones are like a dinosaur attached to an iron lung.

> — **Tom Robinson** (b. 1951),
> British singer/songwriter.

In America, Debbie Harry is the girl next door only if you live in a bad neighborhood.

> — **Roy Carr** (b. 1941),
> British music writer, *New Musical Express.*

I'll be mellow when I'm dead.

> — **Weird Al Yankovic** (b. 1959),
> American rock parodist.

That's what's cool about working with computers. They don't argue, they remember everything and they don't drink all your beer.

> — **Paul Leary**,
> British rock guitarist (1991).

We don't see eye to eye, but we have a common interest: your money.

> — **John Lydon** (b. 1953)(Johnny Rotten),
> British rock singer/songwriter, on a reunion
> tour of the Sex Pistols (1996).

ROMANCE

Music makes one feel romantic — at least it always gets on one's nerves — which is the same thing nowadays.

> — **Oscar Wilde** (1854-1900),
> Irish playwright and novelist.

ROSSINI, GIOACCHINO

Rossini would have been a great composer if his teacher had spanked him enough on his backside.

> — **Ludwig van Beethoven** (1770-1827),
> German composer.

Dear God — here it is, finished, this poor little Mass. ... Little science, some heart, that's all there is to it. Be blessed, then, and grant me a place in Paradise.

> — **Gioacchino Rossini** (1792-1868),
> Italian composer, in an inscription at the end
> of his *Petite Messe Solennelle* (1863).

ROYALTIES

And the royalites went to Royalty

> — **Michael Flanders** (1922-75),
> British humorist and songwriter (with Donald Swann), on
> *Greensleeves* having been written by Henry VIII.

SAXOPHONE

The saxophone is the embodied spirit of beer.
— **Arnold Bennett** (1867-1931),
British novelist (attr.).

SCHOENBERG, ARNOLD

[Schoenberg's *Violin Concerto*] combines the best sound effects of a hen yard at feeding time, a brisk morning in Chinatown and practice hour at a busy music conservatory. The effect on the vast majority of hearers is that of a lecture on the fourth dimension delivered in Chinese.

— **Edwin H. Schloss**,
in the *Philadelphia Record* (December 7, 1940).

SCRIABIN, ALEXANDER

The voluptuous dentist.
— **Aldous Huxley** (1894-1963),
British writer, on Russian composer Alexander Scriabin.

SEX

If sex is such a natural phenomenon, how come there are so many books on how to?
> — **Bette Midler** (b. 1945),
> American singer and actress.

SHAW, GEORGE BERNARD

Bernard Shaw has no enemies, but is intensely disliked by his friends.
> — **Oscar Wilde** (1854-1900),
> Irish playwright and novelist.

The way Bernard Shaw believes in himself is very refreshing in these atheistic days when so many believe in no God at all.
> — **Israel Zangwill**

If you cannot get rid of the family skeleton you might as well make it dance.
> — **George Bernard Shaw** (1856-1950),
> Irish playwright and music critic.

SILENCE

I believe in the discipline of silence and could talk for hours about it.
— **George Bernard Shaw** (1856-1950),
Irish playwright and music critic.

The silent man is the best to listen to.
— **Japanese proverb**

She had lost the art of conversation, but not, unfortunately, the power of speech.
— **George Bernard Shaw** (1856-1950),
Irish playwright and music critic.

SINATRA, FRANK

I wish Frank Sinatra would just shut up and sing.
— **Lauren Bacall** (b. 1924),
American film actress.

Sinatra's idea of Paradise is a place where there are plenty of women and no newspapermen. He doesn't know it, but he'd be better off if it were the other way round.
— **Humphrey Bogart** (1899-1957),
American film actor.

I didn't want to find a horse's head in my bed.
— **Paul Anka** (b. 1941),
Canadian-born American singer/songwriter,
on why he gave *My Way* to Frank Sinatra.

SINGERS ON SINGING

Swans sing before they die — 'twere no bad thing
Should certain persons die before they sing.
— **Samuel Taylor Coleridge** (1772-1834),
British poet, *Epigram on a Volunteer Singer*.

Ya know whatta you do when you shit? Singing, it's the same thing, only up!
— **Enrico Caruso** (1873-1921),
Italian operatic tenor.

All singers have this fault: if asked to sing among friends they are never so inclined; if unasked, they never leave off.
— **Horace** (c. 65-8 BCE) (Quintus Horatius Flaccus),
Italian poet, *Satires* I:3.

Sometimes my voice can make *me* cry.
— **Leonard Cohen** (b. 1934),
Canadian poet/songwriter, quoted by Christopher Jones,
Now magazine (November 3, 1988).

Anything that is too stupid to be spoken is sung.
— **Voltaire** (1694-1778),
French philosopher.

Leonard Cohen gives you the feeling that your dog just died.

— *Q* **magazine**.

You sang like a composer.
— **Jules Massanet** (1842-1912),
French composer, to a tenor
whose singing he disliked.

A base barreltone voice.
— **James Joyce** (1882-1941),
Irish writer, in *Ulysses* (1922).

A vile beastly rottenheaded foolbegotteen brazen-throated pernicious piggish screaming, tearing, roaring, perplexing, spitmecrackle crashmecringle insane ass of a woman is practising howling below-stairs with a brute of a singingmaster so horribly, that my head is nearly off.

— **Edward Lear** (1812-88),
British nonsense writer, in a letter
to Lady Strachey (January 24, 1859).

We've had a request from the audience — but we're going to keep singing anyway.

— **Anon**.

I am saddest when I sing; so are those that hear me; they are sadder ever than I am.
— **Artemus Ward (Charles Farrar Browne)** (1834-67), American journalist and humorist.

My mother used to say that my elder sister has a beautiful contralto voice. This was arrived at not through her ability to reach the low notes — which she could not do — but because she could not reach the high ones.
— **Samuel Butler** (1834-1902), English novelist and essayist, *Note-Books*.

Her voice sounded like an eagle being goosed.
— **Ralph Novak**, on Yoko Ono, in *People* magazine (December 2, 1985).

The higher the voice the smaller the intellect.
— **Ernest Newman** (1869-1959), British music critic and writer (attrib.).

I can hold a note as long as the Chase National Bank.
> — **Ethel Merman** (1909-84),
> American singer and actress.

She was a singer who had to take any note above A with her eyebrows.
> — **Montague Glass** (1877-1934),
> American humorist.

She was a town-and-country soprano of the kind often used for augmenting grief at a funeral.
> — **George Ade** (1866-1944),
> American dramatist and humorist.

Their morals are depraved, they are disreputable purveyors of every kind of vice. ... They also teach but their pedagogy is senseless.
> — **Giralomo Cardano** (1501-76),
> Italian music theorist.

SNORING

Laugh and the world laughs with you. Snore and you sleep alone.
> — **Anthony Burgess** (1917-93),
> British novelist, journalist and composer.

SONG

Song: the licenced medium for bawling in public things too silly or sacred to be uttered in ordinary speech.
— **Oliver Herford**

There was an Old Person of Tring
Who, when somebody asked her sing,
Replied, "Aren't it odd?
I can never tell *God
Save the Weasel* from *Pop Goes the King.*"
— **Anon.**,
in *The New York Times Magazine* (1946).

Once in every lifetime a really beautiful song comes along. ... Until it does, I'd like to do this one.
— **Cliff Richard** (b. 1940),
British singer/songwriter, in his stage act (1983).

SONG TITLES

Blue Turning Grey Over You.
— **Barbershop song title**

If Today Was a Fish, I'd Throw It Back In.
— **Song title**

Drop Kick Me, Jesus, Through the Goal Posts of Life
— **Song title**

I'm So Miserable Without You
It's Almost Like Having You Here.
                    — **Song title by Stephen Bishop**

She Got the Gold Mine,
I Got the Shaft
                    — **Song title by Jerry Reed**

When My Love Comes Back from the Ladies' Room
Will I Be Too Old to Care?
                    — **Song title by Lewis Grizzard**

STRAVINSKY, IGOR

The Rite of Spring

Who wrote this fiendish *Rite of Spring*,
What right had he to write the thing,
Against our helpless ears to fling
Its crash, clash, cling, clang, bing, bang, bing?

And then to call it *Rite of Spring*,
The season when on joyous wing
The birds melodious carols sing
And harmony's in everything!

He who could write the *Rite of Spring*,
If I be right, by right should swing!
                    — *Boston Herald*,
                    (February 6, 1924).

Stravinsky's *Symphony for Wind Instruments* written in memory of Debussy ... was greeted with cheers, hisses, and laughter. I had no idea Stravinsky disliked Debussy so much as this. If my own memories of a friend were as painful as Stravinsky's of Debussy seem to be, I would try to forget him.

— **Ernest Newman** (1869-1959),
British music critic, *Musical Times*, London (July 1921).

[Stravinsky's music is] Bach on the wrong notes.
— **Sergei Prokofiev** (1891-1953),
Russian composer.

The most invigorating sound I heard was a restive neighbor winding his watch.

— **Mildred Norton**,
on a concert of Stravinsky, in the Los Angeles *Daily News*,
(November 12, 1952).

STRING QUARTETS

Most string quartets have a basement and an attic, and the lift is not working.

— **Neville Cardus**,
British music critic, *The Delights of Music* (1966).

SUCCESS

We must believe in luck, for how else can we explain the success of those we don't like?
> — **Jean Cocteau** (1889-1963),
> French poet and artist.

The worst part of success is to try to find someone who is happy for you.
> — **Bette Midler** (b. 1945),
> American singer and actress.

SUICIDE

I tried to commit suicide one day. It was a very Woody Allen-type suicide. I turned on the gas and left all the windows open.
> — **Sir Elton John** (b. 1948),
> British singer/songwriter.

Anybody who has listened to certain kinds of music, or read certain kinds of poetry, or heard certain kinds of performances on the concertina, will admit that even suicide has its brighter aspects.
> — **Stephen Leacock** (1869-1944),
> Canadian humorist and writer.

Taste

No one ever went broke underestimating the taste of the American public.

> — **H.L. Mencken** (1880-1956),
> American journalist and music critic.

I wouldn't say I invented tacky, but I definitely brought it to its present high popularity.

> — **Bette Midler** (b, 1945),
> American singer and actress.

Tchaikovsky, Pyotr Illich

Tchaikovsky's love life was, to put it bluntly, confused.

> — **David W. Barber** (b. 1958),
> Canadian journalist, humorist and musician,
> *Bach, Beethoven and the Boys* (1986)

Friedrich Vischer once observed, speaking of obscene pictures, that they stink to the eye. Tchaikovsky's *Violin Concerto* gives us for the first time the hideous notion that there can be music that stinks to the ear.

> — **Eduard Hanslick** (1825-1904),
> Czech-born Austrian music critic,
> *Neue Freie Presse*, Vienna,
> (December 5, 1881).

Tchaikovsky's *First Piano Concerto*, like the first pancake, is a flop.

> — **Nicolai Soloviev**,
> *Novoye Vremya*, St. Petersburg (November 13, 1875).

TEACHERS

The music teacher came twice each week to bridge the awful gap between Dorothy and Chopin.

> — **George Ade** (1866-1944),
> American dramatist and humorist (attrib.).

Time is a great teacher, but unfortunately it kills all its pupils.

> — **Hector Berlioz** (1803-69),
> French composer.

TENORS

The cast of *Boris Godunov* includes one character called 'An Idiot.' The role is of course sung by a tenor.
— **David W. Barber** (b. 1958),
Canadian journalist, humorist and musician,
When the Fat Lady Sings (1990).

Tenors get women by the score.
— **James Joyce** (1882-1941),
Irish novelist, *Ulysses* (1922).

THEATRE

The theatre is not the place for the musician. When the curtain is up the music interrupts the actor, and when it is down, the music interrupts the audience.
— **Sir Arthur Sullivan** (1842-1900),
British composer of operettas.

TOOTHACHE

Music helps not the toothache.
— **George Herbert** (1593-1633), English poet,
Jacula Prudentum (1651).

TUNING

Gentleman, take your pick!
> — **Sir Thomas Beecham** (1879-1961),
> British conductor, on hearing an
> oboist giving an A for tuning.

UNEMPLOYMENT

The trouble with unemployment is that the minute you wake up in the morning, you're on the job.
> — **Lena Horne** (b. 1917),
> American jazz singer.

I'm a concert pianist. That's a pretentious way of saying I'm unemployed at the moment.
> — **Oscar Levant** (1906-72),
> American actor, composer and pianist,
> in *An American in Paris* (1951).

VAUGHAN WILLIAMS, RALPH

Listening to the *Fifth Symphony* of Ralph Vaughan Williams is like staring at a cow for 45 minutes.
> — **Aaron Copland** (1900-88),
> American composer.

85

I don't know whether I like it, but it's what I meant.
— **Ralph Vaughan Williams** (1872-1958),
British composer, on a passage in
his *Fourth Symphony*.

It looks wrong, and it sounds wrong; but it's right.
— **Ralph Vaughan Williams** (1872-1958),
British composer, also on a passage in
his *Fourth Symphony*.

VERDI, GIUSEPPE

Verdi was intended by nature for a composer, but I am afraid the genius given him — like girls kissing each other — is decided waste of the raw material.
— *Dwight's Journal of Music*,
Boston (July 14, 1855).

VIOLIN

Life is like playing a violin in public and learning the instrument as one goes on.
— **Samuel Butler** (1835-1902),
British writer.

Violinist: a man who is always up to his chin in music.

— **Anon.**

You see, our fingers are circumcised, which gives it a very good dexterity, you know, particularly the pinky.

> — **Itzhak Perlman** (b. 1945),
> Israeli violinist, replying to a comment
> that so many great violinists are Jewish.

Vivaldi, Antonio

All in all, Vivaldi composed about 450 concertos of one sort or another. People who find his music too repetitious are inclined to say that he wrote the same concerto 450 times. This is hardly fair: he wrote two concertos, 225 times each.

> — **David W. Barber** (b. 1958),
> Canadian journalist, humorist and musician,
> in *Bach, Beethoven and the Boys* (1986).

Wagner, Richard

Wagner's music is better than it sounds.

> — **Mark Twain** (1835-1910),
> American writer and humorist
> (also attributed to American humorist Bill Nye, 1850-96).

Wagner has beautiful moments but awful quarter hours.

> — **Gioacchino Rossini** (1792-1868),
> Italian composer.

There is no law against composing music when one has no ideas whatsoever. The music of Wagner, therefore, is perfectly legal.

— **Anon.**,
review in *The National*,
Paris (November 30, 1850).

The prelude to *Tristan and Isolde* sounded as if a bomb had fallen into a large music factory and had thrown all the notes into confusion.

— **J. Stettenheim**,
review in the Berlin *Tribune* (February 6, 1873).

The Prelude to *Tristan und Isolde* reminds one of the old Italian painting of a martyr whose intestines are slowly unwound from his body on a reel.

— **Eduard Hanslick** (1825-1904),
Czech-born Austrian music critic (June 1868).

When a musician can no longer count up to three, he becomes "dramatic," he becomes "Wagnerian."

— **Friedrich Nietszche** (1844-1900),
German philosopher, *The Case of Wagner*.

I love Wagner, but the music I prefer is that of a cat hung up by his tail outside a window and trying to stick to the panes of glass with its paws.

— **Charles Baudelaire** (1821-67),
French poet.

I like Wagner's music better than any other music. It is so loud that one can talk the whole time without people hearing what one says. That is a great advantage.

— **Oscar Wilde** (1854-1900),
Irish novelist, *The Picture of Dorian Gray*.

Wagner is the Puccini of music.

— **J.B. Morton** (1893-1979),
British journalist, who wrote a newspaper
column under the name *Beachcomber*.

We've been rehearsing for two hours — and we're still playing the same bloody tune!

— **Sir Thomas Beecham** (1879-1961),
British conductor, rehearsing Wagner's *Götterdammerung*.

I refused to sing the young Siegfried, because I think he is a bore. I always call him a Wagnerian L'il Abner.
— **Jon Vickers** (b. 1926),
Canadian operatic tenor.

Your Wagner is without pity; he drives the nail slowly into your head with swinging hammer blows.
— **P.A. Fiorentino** (1806-1864).

Wagner is Berlioz without the melody.
— **Daniel Auber** (1782-1871),
French composer, quoted in *Le Ménestrel* (1863).

Tannhäuser is not merely polyphonous, but polycacophonous.
— *Musical World*,
London (October 13, 1855).

After *Lohengrin*, I had a splitting headache, and all through the night I dreamed of a goose.
— **Mily Balakirev** (1837-1910),
Russian composer, in a letter to Vladimir Stasov,
(November 3, 1868).

What time is the next swan?
— **Leo Slezak** (1873-1946),
Czechoslovakian opera tenor, after the mechanical swan left without him during a performance of *Lohengrin*.

Wagner, thank the fates, is no hypocrite. He says right out what he means, and he usually means something nasty.

— **James G. Huneker** (1860-1921),
American music critic and author.

One can't judge Wagner's opera *Lohengrin* after a first hearing, and I certainly don't intend hearing it a second time.

— **Gioacchino Rossini** (1792-1868),
Italian composer.

It is the music of a demented eunuch.

— *Figaro*, Paris,
on the music of Wagner (July 26, 1876).

[Wagner's *Parsifal* is] the kind of opera that starts at six o'clock and after it has been going on for three hours, you look at your watch and it says 6:20.

— **David Randolph** (b. 1914).

Wagner is evidently mad.

— **Hector Berlioz** (1803-1869),
French composer, in a letter (March 5, 1861).

Is Wagner a human being at all? Is he not rather a disease?

— **Friedrich Nietzsche** (1844-1900),
German philosopher.

[The use of leitmotifs] suggests a world of harmless lunatics who present their visiting cards and shout their name in song.

— **Claude Debussy** (1862-1918),
French composer, on the operas of Richard Wagner.

I have witnessed and greatly enjoyed the first act of everything which Wagner created, but the effect on me has always been so powerful that one act was quite sufficient; whenever I have witnessed two acts I have gone away physically exhausted; and whenever I have ventured an entire opera the result has been the next thing to suicide.

— **Mark Twain** (1835-1910),
American journalist and humorist, (1891).

WEDDING MUSIC

Music played at weddings always reminds me of the music played for soldiers before they go into battle.
— **Heinrich Heine** (1797-1856),
German poet and writer.

WOODWINDS

Never let the horns and woodwinds out of your sight; if you can hear them at all, they are too loud.
— **Richard Strauss** (1864-1949),
German composer, giving advice to young conductors.

The chief objection to playing wind instruments it that it prolongs the life of the player.
— **George Bernard Shaw** (1856-1950),
Irish playwright and music critic.

Index

About the Editor

David W. Barber is a journalist and musician and the author of nine books of musical history and humor, including *Bach, Beethoven and the Boys*, *When the Fat Lady Sings* and *Tutus, Tights and Tiptoes*, and two books of literary quotations, *Quotable Alice* and *Quotable Sherlock*. Formerly entertainment editor of the Kingston, Ont., *Whig-Standard* and editor of *Broadcast Week* magazine at the Toronto *Globe and Mail*, he's now a freelance journalist and musician in Toronto. As a composer, his works include two symphonies, a jazz mass based on the music of Dave Brubeck, a *Requiem*, several short choral and chamber works and various vocal-jazz songs and arrangements. He sings with the Toronto Chamber Choir and with his vocal-jazz group, Barber & the Sevilles, which has released a CD, called *Cybersex*.

Selected Bibliography

Bloomsbury Dictionary of Quotations, ed. John Daintith (Bloomsbury, London) 1987, 1996.

Bloomsbury Thematic Dictionary of Quotations, ed. John Daintith et al. (Bloomsbury, London) 1988.

The Book of Rock Quotes, ed. Jonathan Green (Delilah/Putnam, New York), 1982.

A Dictionary of Musical Quotations, ed. Ian Crofton & Donald Fraser (Schirmer Books, New York) 1985.

Lexicon of Musical Invective, ed. Nicholas Slonimsky, 2nd. ed. (University of Washington Press, Seattle and London) 1953, 1965, 1984.

1,911 Best Things Anybody Ever Said, ed. Robert Byrne (Ballentine/Random House, New York and Toronto) 1988.

The Music Lover's Quotation Book: A Lyrical Companion, ed. Kathleen Kimball (Sound And Vision, Toronto) 1990.

The Oxford Dictionary of Modern Quotations, ed. Tony Augarde (Oxford University Press, Oxford and New York) 1991.

A Treasury of Humorous Quotations, ed. Herbert V. Prochnow and Herbert V. Prochnow Jr. (Holt Rinehart, New York) 1969.

The illustrations in this book are reproduced from the *Dover Pictotrial Archive* series *MUSIC, A Pictorial Archive of Woodcuts & Engravings,* by Jim Harter (Dover Publications, New York) 1980.

By David W. Barber, cartoons by Dave Donald

A Musician's Dictionary
preface by Sir Yehudi Menuhin
isbn 0-920151-21-3

Bach, Beethoven and the Boys
Music History as it Ought to Be Taught
preface by Anthony Burgess
isbn 0-920151-10-8

When the Fat Lady Sings
Opera History as it Ought to Be Taught
preface by Maureen Forrester
foreword by Anna Russell
isbn 0-920151-34-5

If it Ain't Baroque
More Music History as it Ought to Be Taught
isbn 0-920151-15-9

Getting a Handel on Messiah
preface by Trevor Pinnock
isbn 0-920151-17-5

Tenors, Tantrums and Trills
An Opera Dictionary from Aida to Zzzz
isbn 0-920151-19-1

Tutus, Tights and Tiptoes
Ballet History as it Ought to Be Taught
preface by Karen Kain
isbn 0-920151-30-2

Better Than It Sounds
A Dictionary of Humorous Musical Quotations

© David W. Barber, 1998

All rights reserved

First published in Canada in April 1998 by
Sound And Vision
359 Riverdale Avenue
Toronto, Canada M4J 1A4
http://www.soundandvision.com
E-mail: musicbooks@soundandvision.com

This printing October 2001
3 5 7 9 11 13 15 - 14 12 10 8 6 4 2

**National Library of Canada
Cataloguing in Publication Data**

ISBN 0-920151-22-1

1. Music - Humor. 2. Music - Quotations, maxims, etc.
I. Barber, David W. (David William), 1958-

ML65.B2355 1998   780'.207   C98-930878-2

Jacket design by Jim Stubbington
Typeset in Century Schoolbook

Printed and bound in Canada

How to Stay Awake
During Anybody's Second Movement
by David E. Walden
cartoons by Mike Duncan
preface by Charlie Farquharson
isbn 0-920151-20-5

How To Listen To Modern Music
Without Earplugs
by David E. Walden
cartoons by Mike Duncan
foreword by Bramwell Tovey
isbn 0-920151-31-0

The Thing I've Played With the Most
Professor Anthon E. Darling Discusses
His Favourite Instrument
by David E. Walden
cartoons by Mike Duncan
foreword by Mabel May Squinnge, B.O.
isbn 0-920151-35-3

I Wanna Be Sedated
Pop Music in the Seventies
by Phil Dellio & Scott Woods
caricatures by Dave Prothero
preface by Chuck Eddy
isbn 0-920151-16-7

The Composers
A Hystery of Music
by Kevin Reeves
preface by Daniel Taylor
isbn 0-920151-29-9

Love Lives of the Great Composers
From Gesualdo to Wagner
by Basil Howitt
isbn 0-920151-18-3

A Working Musician's Joke Book
by Daniel G. Theaker
cartoons by Mike Freen
preface by David W. Barber
isbn 0-920151-23-X

A Note from the Publisher

Sound And Vision is pleased to announce the creation of a new imprint called *Quotable Books*. The first three in the series are illustrated on the back cover. Other titles planned include Quotable Shakespeare, Twain, Wilde, Poe, Blake, Dickens and Quotable Gumshoes. The series will cover the arts, Quotable Opera, Quotable Jazz, and Quotable Metal plus literature and other subject areas including politicians, warlords and statesmen as Julius Ceaser, Winston Churchill, Sir Oliver Cromwell and Franklin D. Roosevelt.

Our books may be purchased for educational or promotional use or for special sales. If you have any comments on this book or any other book we publish or if you would like a catalogue, please write to us at:

Sound And Vision,
359 Riverdale Avenue,
Toronto, Canada M4J 1A4.

Visit our Web site at: www.soundandvision.com. We would really like to hear from you.

We are always looking for suitable original books to publish. If you have an idea or manuscript, please contact us.

Thank you for purchasing or borrowing this book.

Geoffrey Savage
Publisher